Published by Sprout Media, LLC

ISBN-13: 978-1984332134
ISBN-10: 1984332139

Cover Design: Sprout Media, LLC

This title is available for special promotions, premiums, and bulk purchases. For more information, please contact Sprout Media at BizDev@GoSproutMedia.com.

Printed in the United States of America.

HOW TO MARKET YOUR WINERY TO EVERYONE

Tips and Tricks to Market Your Winery to Millennials, Boomers, and Everyone In-Between

1   OUR MANIFESTO

5   MARKETING 101

7   DOES DIGITAL
       MARKETING MATTER?

13   THE BIG 4

19   TIME TO HARVEST

20   REFERENCES

OUR MANIFESTO

We believe the old way of doing things is over. With the advent of a mobile device in everyone's hand, we are in the midst of a once-every-50-years shift in consumption.

We believe in doing things differently. Not to be different, but to stand out.

We freaking love brands. That can be La Croix, Summerset Winery, Wendy's, Lowry Leather, Horizon Line Coffee, or any other product or place providing great experiences. A brand is what people feel. It's what they aspire to. It's who they are and what they love.

Every business has a unique story to tell. And we work to build, maintain, and expand those unique brand stories.

WHAT IS YOUR STORY?

The brands we build are setup to redefine expectations, inspire action, grow the business, and develop and cultivate long-term relationships with your clients and customers.

Our mission is to build stories that engage and brands that last.

We feel there is an incredible opportunity for wineries to embrace digital marketing once and for all. We aren't just talking about websites, we're talking social networks, email marketing, and video, amongst other things.

MARKETING ISN'T JUST

a website ...
a Facebook page ...
a logo ...
or a brochure.

Think about it. It's a Wednesday afternoon and a group of friends wants to grab a drink after a long day of work. How will they know where to go? Their immediate thought it probably the latest hip bar or a nearby hangout. Why can't that be your wine tasting room or your patio on a beautiful fall evening? Just then, one of the friends says, "I got a text message from (insert your winery name here) this morning." She quickly pulls up the text on their phone and the coupon is waiting for them to use as a group. Another group member quickly pulls up Instagram and tells the others that the winery looks perfect and they notice you just opened a brand wine! Together, they all decide your winery is the where they are going to meet!

EVERYTHING
IS MARKETING.

This scenario can not happen unless you have a text message campaign designed to automatically send a text during key moments. Or an e-mail campaign set to remind your fans of your great patio and happy hour specials. It also doesn't happen unless your winery is active on Instagram in a smart and strategic way.

Here's a fact to ferment on: Over 47% of millennials make purchase decisions based on what they see on social media.[1]

MARKETING 101

- Marketing isn't a website.
- Marketing isn't a Facebook page.
- Marketing isn't a logo.
- And marketing isn't a brochure.

Marketing is all those things and so much more. It's the experience customers have. It's the promise of the brand. It's content. It's advertising. It's your staff.

> ## MISSION
>
> *is what you are all about.*

Marketing is everything you do to market your business product or service.

Some of the world's best companies understand that to its core. Take Apple for example[2]; their company mission is: To make a contribution to the world by making tools for the mind that advance humankind.

NASA mission[3]: to pioneer the future in space

exploration, scientific discovery and aeronautics research.

Adirondack Winery mission[4]: To provide our customers with delicious, award-winning, quality wines that are all hand-crafted locally.

And Ladoga Ridge Winery[5]: To offer each of our guests an inviting and fun atmosphere where they can Relax & Reflect, while enjoying our high-quality, affordable, hand-crafted wines, surrounded by the natural beauty of our vineyards and the unsurpassed service of our staff.

And now you. What is your mission? Is it to provide a great experience at local prices? To be the premier winery in the region? Or even bigger to be a steward of the craft in all ways and to provide an incredible experience any time someone comes for a glass.

As a winery, your marketing consists of everything: your staff, your photography, your videos, your website, your tastings, your emails, your social media, your advertising … the list goes on and on.

DOES DIGITAL MARKETING MATTER?

You're damn right it matters!

Before we dive into why it matters, let us ask you this question:

Do you want to be just like the radio executives who didn't believe television was here to stay?

Do you really believe digital media; websites, Facebook, Google, and text messaging aren't here to stay? And if you do believe they are here to stay, do you want your competitors to beat you there; a place where everyone is spending their time and money?

The way we consume has always been changing and evolving. It is just hard to see because we change with it.

Check out this map:

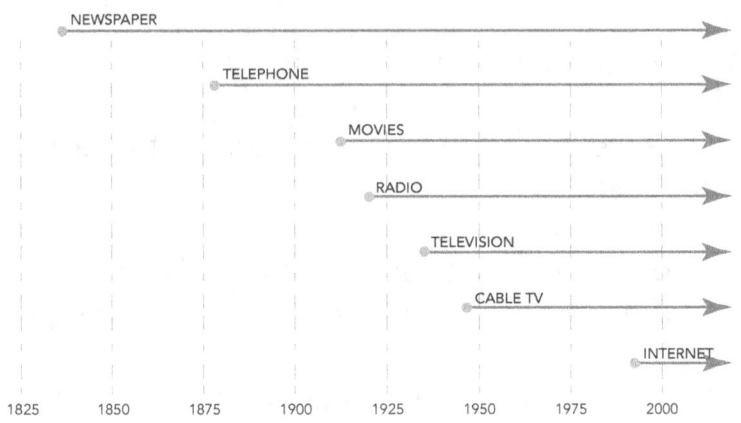

At the end of 2017, we were consuming data in vastly and dramatically different ways than even just a few years ago.

Various data sources and research studies report that adults in the United States spend between 11 and 13 hours per day with media of various types.[6] What that tells us is that adults are inundated with content throughout the day; morning, noon, and night. What that doesn't tell us is how.

The majority or users are single-platform users. At any given moment, users may be watching television, using their mobile device, and typing on their laptops at the same time. Our media time is no longer finite, but rather multi-dimensional, and therefore, when marketing, the strategy for any company must always be to find where the attention is; and grab it!

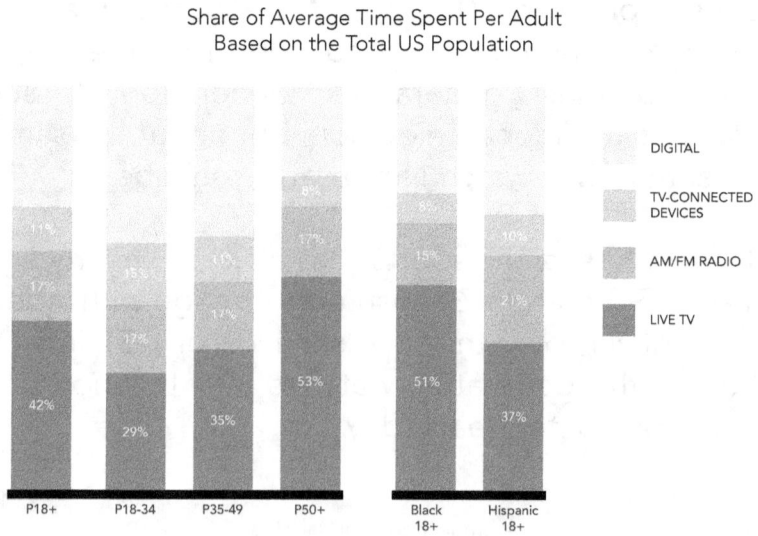

Share of Average Time Spent Per Adult
Based on the Total US Population

DIGITAL

TV-CONNECTED DEVICES

AM/FM RADIO

LIVE TV

P18+ | P18-34 | P35-49 | P50+ | Black 18+ | Hispanic 18+

With the rate of television consumption still around four hours a day, we still watch a significant amount of television. And that four hours amounts to nearly 33% of all media consumption in the United States; a dominant portion of all media time.

But here is the challenge with television:

Obviously our eyes are on the screen during the live action, but what happens during commercials? For a lot of viewers, that means a second screen engagement; and thus, television takes a back seat.

Merge that with the rapid rise in mobile internet use, (projected to become 26% of global media consumption in 2019)[7], and the possibilities for marketers and content producers are endless.
The youngest generation, Generation Z, still watches traditional television, but not at the same level that they watch Netflix and YouTube.

Trifecta Research reports that 59%[8], or nearly six-in-ten Generation Z consumers engage with video content via "over-the-top" services, or OTT. In fact, 70% of this generation watches over two hours of YouTube content each day.

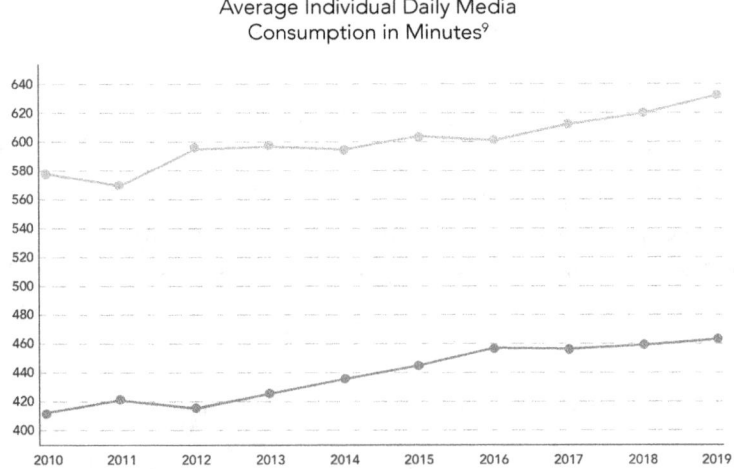

Average Individual Daily Media Consumption in Minutes[9]

Overall, the marketing game is all about attention and that's where a lot of agencies and companies have missed out. Attention is and always will be the key to any marketing strategy.

Just because you put up a billboard and 10,000 cars drive by every day doesn't mean that you have their attention. The same can be said for television ads, print ads, digital banner ads, and on and on.

Here is a final stat on attention you need to know: According to a recent America Wine Generations Report, 63% of Gen X wine drinkers have posted about wine on social media.[10]

You must always ask yourself, "Do I have their attention?" Of course, there are levels of attention and each level has a different tactic, but if you don't have their attention at the right moment, you've already lost.

 # THE BIG 4

What does this all mean for your winery and/or tasting room?

While every winery's strategy and tactics will vary, one thing will remain constant: Your marketing strategy must be focused on providing valuable information and content on the right platforms, in the right format, and at the right moment.

Attention is the scarce commodity that will connect the Big 4 elements together. The overall objective is to keep visitors returning for more of your content and then to visit and frequent your winery.

How exactly do you do that?

By Following the Big 4 of Winery Marketing.

First and foremost, a website. We're not talking about a website just to have a website. We're talking about a website where people can click and get all the information they could ever want about your winery. A updated calendar, the ability to book a party, sign up for your email and text message list, and helping visitors find your brewery on social media.

Your website should be where you "drive" all of your customers. A place to communicate with every single one of your customers about your winery, your food and drinks, and reinforce and remind them why they should visit!

It's 2017, everyone has a website. The small businesses, companies, and in your case, wineries that really stand out have bright, user friendly websites; mobile too! (That means, don't build your site on Wix!)

A major piece of websites is their Search Engine Optimization (SEO). In layman's terms: SEO is the technology behind Google search results. There is a strategy to ensuring your website is found first among your competitors.

And that is the goal: to be the first thing wine lovers in your area find and think about.

SOCIAL

When we think of wineries we think of something cool, unique, fun, and different. All of these things bundled together and you can get some amazing pictures and videos.

Social media platforms, like Facebook, Instagram, Snapchat, and the like, are easy channels to provide fans and friends alike with incredible access to your winery and vineyard.

Just picture this for your tasting room and winery:

- Behind the scenes photos
- Someone in the vineyard showing how the process of harvesting works
- A live look at the fermentation of the latest Concord
- A guide on how to taste the unique notes of your grapes

All of these pieces of content are designed to engage your users; grab their attention and drive them to a specific action.

And each winery is different. Some places crush content and engagement on Facebook. Some are owning Snapchat. At the end of 2017, Instagram was gaining the highest engagement rates for breweries over Facebook and Twitter.

Social content is not as simple as taking a picture and posting it. There needs to be a reason for the content. There is nothing worse than posting content for no reason when you have someone's attention, and wasting it.

> *RIGHT MESSAGE.*
> *RIGHT TIME.*

EMAIL & TEXT MESSAGE

When it comes to experiential businesses, Sprout Media believes that most businesses have yet to tap into the power of e-mail marketing. Sure, companies send updates and news, but e-mail has the power to drive business results when you least expect it.

All marketing, e-mail & text message marketing is all about one simple concept:

RMRT:
Right Message at the Right Time

One of the worst things marketers do with e-mail is blast. Just shoot emails as often as possible because … eventually … someone will bite! But that's not smart or strategic. That's just random. But marketing and sales aren't random.

The correct approach is to learn from your customers.

For example, have you ever signed up for a clothing company's mailing list after a purchase, only to be marketed to for weeks and months and years, but there is just random content in the emails. Worse yet is that the emails are still coming into your inbox at the same cadence as they did when you first signed up even though you haven't purchased anything since that first sale.

Long-gone are the days of just blasting emails to your list (even though many companies still take that approach). As you get to know your fans, you're going to learn more about them; are they every week visitors or do they come just every month or so. You're going to begin to understand what brings them in and why they come back.

When you have that contextual information, that is when you can really make some magic happen in your e-mail (or text message) marketing efforts.

Here is an idea for you: You have a list of people who are semi-frequent visitors and you also know Tuesdays are a slow afternoon for your tasting room. So, instead of hoping customers come in, you inspire them to visit. You let them know you have something new and exciting for them, and those who come in get something "on the house." It's a fun way to engage and doesn't take much from your end.

EVENTS

Every moment at a winery can become an "event." These are not events like weddings and anniversary parties at the clubhouse, but rather experiences together with friends and family.

- Tasting a new wine
- Toasting a new job
- Celebrating a holiday
- Celebrating a beautiful day
- Or just celebrating a great tasting glass of wine

All of these things are experiences, moments, events that evoke an emotional response to your customers and potential customers. When we think of marketing, it all comes back to RMRT (Right Message, Right Time).

We call these micro-moments. Yes, running a brewery is busy and hard. But when someone connects with your brand on a deeper level, you will have made a potential customer for life.

♀ TIME TO HARVEST

In a study from the Journal of Applied Social Psychology, researchers found that waiters could increase their tips by 23 percent by the simple act of returning to tables with a second set of mints. So do mints have magic powers? Not exactly but the researchers concluded that the mints created the feeling of a personalized experience among the customers who received them.

Therefore, it was the personalized service received that made them enjoy their experience so much more. Whether your visitors are first-timers at your winery or long-time fans, the experience matters; online, before they arrive, their glass of ine, and their time with you.

Make a memorable experience each-and-every time and your marketing will take care of itself.

REFERENCES

1. https://www.forbes.com/sites/jimmyrohampton/2017/05/03/ does-social-media-influence-millennials-shopping- decisions/#77a7c22b4cf3
2. https://www.inc.com/jim-schleckser/apple-s-boring-mission- statement-and-what-we-can-learn-from-it.html
3. http://www.ucsusa.org/our-work/center-science-and- democracy/promoting-scientific-integrity/at-nasa-earth-is- removed.html#.WhLFxbQ-eRs
4. https://www.adirondackwinery.com/About-Us/Mission-- Values
5. http://www.ladogaridgewinery.com/mission_statement
6. https://www.emarketer.com/Article/US-Adults-Now-Spend- 12-Hours-7-Minutes-Day-Consuming-Media/1015775
7. https://www.zenithmedia.com/26-of-media-consumption- will-be-mobile-in-2019/
8. http://trifectaresearch.com/wp-content/uploads/2015/09/ Generation-Z-Sample-Trifecta-Research-Deliverable.pdf
9. https://www.recode.net/2017/5/30/15712660/media- consumption-zenith-mobile-internet-tv
10. http://www.bauerhaus.com/marketing-wine-to-moms-on- social-media/